TRIBULATION TO VICTORY: BIRTH OF A QUEEN

SHANNON SPRUILL

Copyright © 2018 by Shannon Spruill

All rights reserved.

No part of this book may be reproduced in any form or by any electronic or mechanical means, including information storage and retrieval systems, without written permission from the author, except for the use of brief quotations in a book review.

Shannon Spruill/SMS Write On Publishing, LLC.

3843 Union Road, Suite 15, #141 Cheektowaga, NY. 14225
www.smswriteonpublishingllc.com www.authorshannonspruill.com

Editor CaTyra Polland Polland Enterprises, LLC
www.pollandllc.com

ISBN 978-1732023413

This book is dedicated to my son, Brian M. Spruill, Forever in my heart!

CHAPTER 1

Thinking about school was a reminder of just how ugly I felt. Children take to heart the things other children tell them. First grade, tall, and in the back of the line. Being at the end of the line represented a negative image in my mind. My first desire was to be short because it seemed all the pretty girls were shorter than me. My second biggest desire was to belong. Belonging represented love and who would not want to be loved. I was never accepted into the cool groups. I was always on the outside looking in. The boys never hesitated to let me know just how ugly I was while being ignored by the girls. At an early age, I knew what it meant to be lonely. I developed low self-esteem and a need to belong allowed me to accept things I should not have tolerated. These emotions are a story that many have told, but understanding the depth of these feelings is a whole new story by itself. Many feel that these are things that some children deal with, but as time goes by, they grow up and those issues disappear. Wrong–these are issues that can always be a part of your life, and can develop into other problems. At the age of 9, the mirror became my obsession. I would look in the mirror and I did not like what was staring back at me.

I grew up in Brooklyn, New York. My grandmother raised me and I called her mom. My father died when I was four years old. But my mother was still living. I often wondered why my mother had abandoned us. My mother had a mental breakdown and was not capable of raising my sister and me. You know my thoughts went straight to, "Can I have a mental breakdown like my mother did?" As a little girl, I remember a woman who would always visit us on birthdays and Christmas. She always brought us gifts. Around the age of eight, I began to wonder about that woman. Could she be our mom? Was it possible? After the visits stopped, I found out that undoubtedly that was our mother. My grandmother was the best mother you could ask for, but there were still questions.

CHAPTER 2

My first day of school I wore a green and white dress and black patent leather shoes. My mother made this dress and most of my clothes. I thought I looked very nice for my first day at school, but my classmates quickly let me know that I was not cool. Even now I have never forgotten that day. Second, third, fourth and fifth grades were pretty much the same feelings of not belonging. I was often teased about how I looked and about the clothes I wore. I never told my mother because at a young age I understood that my mother was an excellent provider and she made sure we had all the things that we needed. She was an excellent seamstress and made many of our dresses for school. My peers had no appreciation for this and not buying the more fashionable styles made me the brunt of cruel jokes. I know that these experiences were not unique, but I believe the feelings that are harbored, as a result, are individual. In the sixth grade, I began to look at myself in the mirror. I wanted to see what other people saw. We all look in the mirror for various reasons; to make sure our makeup is correct, to make sure our hairstyle is cute, but do we exam ourselves as if we are looking at another person? I wanted to be that other person seeing me. I began to see an image I did not like. During this time, I also developed an interest in boys. Unfortunately, that interest was one-sided. Boys took no interest in me. Instead, they made fun of me. I often found myself in front of the mirror pretending to talk with some boy who found me attractive. It was around this time that I met Beverly, the most popular girl in school. I thought this was cool to be associated with Beverly. It was as if some of her would rub off on me. Every boy in school liked Beverly, and all the girls envied her. She sat beside me in math class. One day she told me that some kids were coming to her house after school and asked if I would like to come. I quickly, without thinking, responded yes.

  I needed to come up with a believable lie to tell my mother because she would not let me go to someone's house she has never met, especially if she never met their parents. I told my mother I needed to go to the library to work on a project for school. I hated lying to my mother, but I honestly felt like I had no choice. Finally, I felt like I belonged. I quickly learned that new relationships are not always what they seem. I realized that I was being used. Beverly needed someone to do her math homework and guess who she chose? Even though I knew I was being used, I continued to hang around Beverly. Funny thing was the reflection in the mirror was still the same.

   I developed a fear of walking past a group of people by myself. It was very common to find kids gathered together in groups after school on the street where I lived. If I didn't have my sister to walk home with, I am not sure I could have made it down the road. I began to hate going to the corner store by myself for fear there would be a group of kids along my route. At the time, I couldn't understand or explain this fear. It was a paralyzing fear. I would sometimes walk the opposite direction and take an out of the way route just to avoid the crowd.

      I hung around Beverly all the way through the 7th grade. I always maintained excellent grades. I skipped the 8th grade altogether and went straight to the 9th grade in high school. One other aspect of my life at this time was my religion. I was raised going to church every Sunday. Around the age of 13, I began to have conversations with God. I was not saved, but I needed answers or just someone to talk to and God was my choice. I often wondered if God really loved me and if He did, then why would I look in the mirror and cry. Shouldn't I look in the mirror and smile? I was so confused and conflicted. I tried to chalk it up to growing pains, and that I was experiencing what every pre-teen goes through. But something was happening. Something was definitely wrong. High school was much tougher. My first year, I was able to perform academically with my peers, but it was harder to fit in. Because I got skipped to the 9th grade, I did not have my sister the first two years of high school. One ugly experience I recall is being surrounded by six girls in the bathroom. They forced me to smoke what I thought was marijuana. I never had a desire to try drugs but under the threat of bodily harm I began to smoke the marijuana joint. My tormentors thought that this was the funniest thing and then one of the girls said to me, "You know you just smoked angel dust." I just wanted to escape. After the girls left the bathroom, I gathered up my belongings and headed to my math class. Once I was in my math class, I could not focus on the teacher because I started seeing and hearing things. I decided to put my head down on my desk and close my eyes. This seemed to make things worse. I felt like I could literally feel my heart pounding as if it were about to explode. The bell rang and class was over but I could not move. I lifted my head, and the room started turning. I put my head back down. My teacher came over and asked what was wrong. I told a lie and said I was just feeling sick and dizzy. She offered to walk me to the nurse's office, but I told her I could not steady myself to stand. They sent for a wheelchair to take me to the nurse's office. They called my mother, and she had my aunt come and pick me up from school. A series of doctors' appointments followed and no one could figure out what was wrong. I was eventually given a clean bill of health by my doctor. I never told anyone what happened. This is when my fear of passing by a group of people intensified. If I saw a group of kids congregating, I would walk in the opposite direction and take an alternate route to class. I had no one to explain my fears to, and I felt so alone. My family and school teachers often told me how intelligent I was and that if I applied myself, I could achieve greatness. I just couldn't imagine myself becoming anyone of significance. Regardless of how intelligent I was, there were too many negative images floating around inside of my head. I began to question my sanity; did a sane person have conversations with their image in the mirror? Did a sane person experience unexplained fears that gripped their whole being? There has to be something insane about what I was experiencing. I believed I cried every day and sometimes for no reason. I started to believe that when I got older, I would not be able to cry because of all the tears that have flowed down my cheeks already. I would get home from school and go to the bathroom and lock the door. I would spend time just crying. Crying for me was like a cleansing that rid my body of all the negative feelings and experiences. After crying I actually would have a brief moment of feeling good. For a brief moment I felt like there was nothing I could not conquer. Because crying produced good feelings, it was as if I needed to cry every day. Through all of this I continued to perform well in school. I also picked up a bad habit around this time, smoking cigarettes. My grandmother smoked, so it was easy to steal a few of her cigarettes. When I first starting smoking, it was to be cool like everyone else. It later developed into an addiction. My second year in high school I began to make some friends. I also began to have male friends, but it was always just friends. In the 11th grade I started dating Andre. Andre was very popular and to my disbelief he showed an interest in me. At least this was what I wanted to believe. I quickly became educated in the motives of young men. I also learned that I was not his only girlfriend and definitely not the more important of the two. The other girlfriend was beautiful. Her complexion was flawless. She could have been a model. I did not believe I could compete with her on any level. The only way I could compete was to put out. This was my first heartbreak. Back to the mirror to try to understand why I am not good enough.

CHAPTER 3

As I entered into my senior year in high school, I suddenly noticed that more young men took notice of me. I really felt like there had to be a catch because why would young men be interested in me when there were plenty of pretty girls in my school. I did enjoy the attention, but I was always cautious. It was then that I realized that I had problems. Depression was the first self-diagnosis, and I realized that maybe I needed to talk with someone. My mood was often gloomy and I would cry for no apparent reason at all. It was so difficult for me to think about talking to someone. I really did not want to face hearing someone telling me that I was crazy. I stopped going to church by my senior year in high school, but I did continue my conversations with God. I truly felt that I could confide in God. I needed someone to tell me they understood. Unfortunately, I had not learned to communicate with God. To be able to hear him and understand his will. I was not able to enjoy and experience life as a child or teenager.

One of the darkest days of my life is when I learned just how cruel the world could be. I was walking home from school one day and a man complimented me and I was so caught up with the attention that I was receiving that I did not notice the knife. I was forced to the rooftop of an apartment building. In order to escape, I went to a deep mental closet where I was safe from harm. I was not there on that rooftop. I was in a dark closet hiding from bad people. I was a child looking for safety from the bad monster. I can't provide details because I mentally escaped. This is the first time in my life that I mentioned that dark day. I could not tell anyone because there was a part of me that felt like it was my fault. After the man left, I sat on that rooftop for hours. I was void of any feeling, just completely numb. I tried to make sense of what happened to me. I had no one to tell me things are going be alright. It is also times like this I longed for my father. When I think of a father, I think of a protector. At that moment, I truly needed my protector. On top of all that I was dealing with, I had to deal with getting in trouble for coming home late. I could not tell my mother what happened, so I dealt with the punishment. Afterwards, off to the bathroom to look at my reflection in the mirror and cry for a while. This cry was not a cleansing cry; it was a truly painful cry.

After I graduated from high school, I went to community college and discovered a whole new world. I got some news that really scared me. I went to a routine doctor's appointment, and the doctor discovered a lump in my breast. Eighteen years old and there was a lump in my breast. Of course, cancer was the first thought that ran through my head. Oh my God, was I going to die? I had never experienced such a gripping fear. Before I went to take tests, I went straight to the library to educate myself. I wanted to know everything about breast cancer. I needed to know what my chances were and if I had a chance at survival. My doctor told me not to panic, but how do you tell an 18-year-old that she has a lump in her breast and not to worry. The doctor scheduled a mammogram, and the mammogram was not conclusive, so they also scheduled a biopsy. I will never forget hearing, "It is just a cyst." Before I could finish celebrating, I got the news that my pap smear was abnormal. My father died at the age of 24 and I always had a fear that I would die young as well. This type of news from the doctor did not help my fears. I went to see my doctor, and he said they discovered abnormal cells and there was a possibility that they were cancerous. He recommended I undergo a procedure called a Cone Biopsy. A Cone Biopsy is a surgical procedure that removes a cone-shaped piece of the cervix. A Cone Biopsy is done if a pap smear indicated moderate-to-severe cell changes. As part of the treatment, the abnormal tissue is removed. A Cone Biopsy can also aid in diagnosing cervical cancer and what stage it is at. This was the very first time that I was in the hospital and my very first surgical procedure. After the surgery, the doctor would send a tissue sample to the lab to determine if I had cancer and if all abnormal cells were removed. This was an extremely overwhelming experience. I overplayed scenario after scenario in my head. Was I going to live, or was I going to die? Was I going to suffer? Was I being punished for something? So many questions and I didn't seem to have definitive answers. The morning of the surgery was just so surreal. I didn't remember much before I went into the operating room, but I remember waking up and feeling some minor discomfort. The doctor came to see me and told me that I had cervical dysplasia (a precancerous condition). I still had to wait for the lab to confirm no cancer. But I survived and felt like I could start living again. After this, my mood continued to be gloomy, and I had frequent bouts of unexplained crying. I should have been happy, but for some reason, happiness escaped me. I finally decided that maybe I should see a doctor about how I was feeling. I wondered if I could truly open up to a stranger about what I was feeling. Somehow, I thought it would be easier with a stranger than with someone I knew. I made a call to my doctor, and she recommended a psychiatrist that would accept my insurance. The worst part about this recommendation was that the doctor's office was inside of a well-known drug rehab center. I was not very comfortable about the environment and not sure I could really open up but I was determined to meet with this doctor. I sat inside the doctor's office waiting to be seen. Well, when the doctor walked in, I automatically knew I would not be able to open up to this man. I could not deal with the thought of a stranger passing judgment on me. So, I spent the next thirty minutes telling him what I thought he wanted to hear. He just listened and then said he would set up additional meetings. Before I walked out the door, I knew I would not be back. What a waste of time. I decided right then I could beat this, and I did not need a shrink. I needed to move on.

CHAPTER 4

My mother often warned me to be careful who I associate with. I remember my mother saying many times, "never be so anxious to run with the fast crowd." Once I moved out on my own, I thought I could ignore my mother's advice. Even after having my first child, those same fears of rejection and not belonging continued to haunt me. I did start hanging around with the fast crowd and it almost cost me my life. One evening while I was with my new cool friends standing in front of my apartment building, one of the guys jumped up and knocked me to the ground. The only thing I saw as I hit the ground was a flash of light. As I got up from the ground, I realized that the flash of light was from a gunshot. The bullet was not meant for me, but for one of the girls that were standing right next to me. No one was hurt, and it turned out to be a jealous boyfriend. At that point, it became clear that I needed to evaluate the crowd I associated with.

I found myself unable to take work serious and my mood would constantly change. I was a great master of disguise. Most people who met me and knew me thought I had it together. People came to me for advice because they admired my strength. No one had any idea of just how mixed up I truly was. My intelligence and interest in psychology made it easy for me to wear my disguise. I have always had an interest in human behavior and learning the complexities of the human mind was intriguing but I could not apply it to my own life. Sometimes I just wanted to scream at people and say, "YOU DON'T KNOW WHO I AM!" But instead, I tried to deal with my problems in silence. I became so extremely tired and all I wanted was peace. I wanted no more crying, no more hurt and no more loneliness. I wanted to close my eyes and sleep. The thought of suicide became a solution. There is a theory that people who are depressed sleep a lot. Well sleeping for me was sometimes the most peaceful time in my life, so I welcomed sleep. Regardless of what I went through, I was always concerned about the needs and feelings of others. With that being said, when I contemplated suicide, my first thought was how would it affect my loved one? I really didn't want to take my own life, but that thought of peaceful sleep was so very tempting. I rode the subway to work and there were times I would be riding to work and just sit there as the train would ride by my stop. I would ride the train to the end of the line. There were days I would ride the subway all day long. I would just look at the different people and try to imagine what their thoughts were. I felt so alone and isolated. Was this the way other people felt or was I abnormal? There were times that I felt motivated and determined to make a positive change, but those were short-lived feelings. Another odd thing was as I got older I never had a problem making friends and I got along very well with other people. My friends never made me feel inadequate around them, but the image in the mirror constantly haunted me. Now that I look back I was ripe for the picking for any young man just looking for a woman to string along and use. It was around this time that I met Kenny. He instantly took an interest in me. I later figured out that his interest in me was all about getting me in bed. But even though I knew this, getting that attention was more important to me. We saw each other often but most of the time it was my efforts. I was 19 years old at the time and I was living on my own. I was doing pretty well for myself at this age working for a legal book publisher as a secretary. Then one day I realized that my period had not arrived. Could I be? No not me. But what if I was? Just the thought made me scared but yet there was a slight moment of excitement. Pregnant! Wow, was it possible? I called Kenny and asked him to come over and I told him I was pregnant. I should not have been surprised by his response. "Are you sure it is mine?" and "Do you plan on getting an abortion?" At this moment, I felt so hurt and alone. My response was "with or without you I will have this baby."

He did not move in with me but would come by frequently and spend the night. One evening he came by with a female. Her name was Angela; someone he said was his cousin. She would come by with him on the weekends and he would always leave with her to take her home. Funny thing was when he left with her I would not see him for the rest of the weekend. Well, his brother informed me that they had no cousin named Angela. Need I explain? Well, it was time for me to move on from this relationship. This was the beginning of my journey as a single parent. My grandmother was there for me every step of the way including the delivery room. There I was with a son named Derek.

Kenny's family had no interest in being in the baby's life. Only one of his brothers kept in touch with me. Raising my son was made less difficult because my grandmother helped me a lot. My son was my world. I could not believe that I was a mother. I had someone to love and someone to love me back. During the first year after Derek was born, I didn't have a lot of time to concentrate on myself, so I didn't cry as much and didn't look in the mirror as much.

CHAPTER 5

I was in the process of purchasing all new furniture for my apartment and decided to give my living room couch to my ex-boyfriend's brother, Joe. I stayed in contact with him and his wife Donna. They came by on Wednesday to pick up the couch, and Joe had a friend with him. His friend instantly caught my attention. I pulled Donna aside and invited them to come over on Friday and to extend the invitation to their friend. They all showed up on Friday and we played cards into the early morning.

That morning Esau proposed to me. I was in a state of shock because I was a firm believer that there was no such thing as love at first sight. Someone thought I was worthy to be a wife? Did he have a motive or could I have truly found love? Well, to the surprise of my family and friends (myself included), I said, "Yes" to Esau, and we were married four months later. Esau and I have now been married for approximately 32 years. These 32 years have been about discovery, healing and a new me.

Early in our marriage, there were the normal struggles. The biggest struggle in our relationship was control. Esau was from a very traditional background with the belief that the woman follows her husband. I believed that if I work, I have an equal amount of say in the marriage. We struggled but through the years mutual respect developed. Esau made me feel like a queen. He never hesitated to tell me how beautiful I was, but unfortunately, I found it hard to believe he was sincere. I didn't know how to take his compliments. I often found myself questioning his sincerity. You would think that at this point in my life I would not have unexplained crying and I could look in the mirror and see beauty. The compliments my husband showered me with were not helping. Somehow it made things worst. I would look in the mirror and try to see what he saw and I just couldn't see it. During my first year of marriage, I became pregnant again. We had another boy, Brian Matthew.

CHAPTER 6

Esau and I were meeting for lunch one afternoon and he spotted a woman who he thought looked just like me. I could not believe I was looking at the woman who would visit on birthdays and Christmas. Did I really want to uncover this unknown part of my life? Behold, this was my mother. The woman who gave birth to me and it was like we were meeting for the first time. I was filled with mixed emotions. I was glad to come face to face with my mother, but there was some deep-seated animosity brewing. Why or how could you walk away from your children? As a mother, I could not imagine walking away from my children. I needed to know but on the other hand; I didn't want to know. I had so much going on in my head; I didn't know if I had room for this.

I went up to Erminie, and she instantly knew who I was. She was a very pleasant woman and there was a sense of gentleness about her. She was glad to see me and we exchanged phone numbers and promised to meet for lunch. It turns out that she had been working in the same building that I worked in. Was this God orchestrating life? We met for lunch and I could not imagine this woman abandoning her children. I decide at this point I would not judge her and I would let her tell me her story when she was ready. I believe everyone deserves a chance to make things right. Everyone's capacity to deal with problems is different. She explained to me that after my father's death; she had a nervous breakdown. She admitted herself into the hospital. It was at this point I stopped her and told her I did not want to hear any more. I told her, "I just want to get to know the person you are today and see what can develop from this point on." From that point, I got to know the woman who was my mother. I made it very clear to her that I would never know my grandmother as anything other than my mother. She respected that and did not ask for anything but a chance at a relationship. I got to know Erminie the person. She was a very sweet, a humble and a generous person. My children warmed up to her quickly and Esau hit it off with her from the beginning. It was not as if I found my mother, but it was more like I found a dear and precious friend. This worked for me and I believe it worked for Erminie as well.

CHAPTER 7

*E*sau lived in the Bronx when we first met. After we married, he moved to Brooklyn with me. We decided we needed a change of scenery and decided to move to Atlanta, Georgia. This was a good move for Esau because most of his family was in Atlanta. We stayed in Atlanta for a year before moving to Buffalo, New York. We left Atlanta because the cost of living was high. I had family in Buffalo and the cost of living was much lower than Atlanta or Brooklyn. We also enjoyed the slower pace compared to a busy big city. Our second year in Buffalo we had our 3rd child and named him Patrick James. Then I decided to get my tubes tied because we only wanted three children. I love all three of my sons but I never had a desire to have children. I was glad I had all boys because girls were high maintenance.

After having three children I decided it was time for me to dedicate some time to set goals in my life. I did not want to stay home and just take care of kids. My first step was to enroll in school and get my Associates Degree. I felt good about myself and felt like my life was on track. I still had occasional bouts of crying but I was very focused on school. I was in my last semester of school and had maintained a perfect 4.0 GPA. But then there came another scare. About a year after Patrick was born I started feeling ill. The first thing I noticed was my energy level. I literally had no energy. I was constantly tired. Next, I started to notice the formation of a large lump in the middle of my neck in the throat area. It was time for a doctor's appointment. I was not too concerned because I thought maybe it was some type of swollen gland and I probably had some type of viral infection. The Doctor confirmed my suspicions. He told me I had a viral infection and it should clear up in a couple of days. Well, two weeks later nothing seemed to change. I was in the bathroom combing my hair and noticed a big patch of hair that came out in my hand. This horrified me. What was going on?

This same day I was on my way to school and

seated on the bus. My stop was coming up, and I rang the bell to get off the bus. I attempted to get up and my legs would not move. I was so scared and could not understand why I could not move my legs. I rode past my stop in fear. I finally gathered the courage to tell the woman sitting next to me that I was feeling extremely ill and asked if she could please help me get off the bus. Once she helped me to my feet, I was able to walk. I immediately went to a phone booth, called my doctor and made an appointment.

      I went to see my doctor the following day. After blood work and a physical exam, he told me to get dressed. As I was getting dressed, I noticed he was writing in his prescription pad. I asked what was wrong with me and he stated he could not find anything physically wrong with me. I told him that must be a mistake because there was still a lump in my throat, my hair was falling out and I was rapidly losing weight. His response was "it is stress related." I asked him what the prescription was for and he told me, "I am sending you to see a psychiatrist." When the doctor left the room, the only thing I could do was cry. I felt so humiliated because I knew something was wrong with me but I was made to feel like I was crazy. I left the doctor's office in a daze. I could not understand what was happening to me. I went home and as always Esau tried his best to comfort me.

Later that afternoon I went to see a friend named Jackie. Jackie said her mother was worried about me and thought something was wrong. Jackie's mother saw me several times and had noticed the gaunt look and the weight loss. She gave Jackie the name and phone number of her doctor. She had a lot of confidence in her doctor and thought he may be able to help me. I started to throw the phone number away, but instead, I put the piece of paper, with the name and phone number on it, in my purse. It was like there was some type of divine intervention. The following morning, I called the phone number and made an appointment with Dr. Berman. What did I have to lose? I just wanted to feel better. Before my appointment with Dr. Berman, his office called and had me go and take a blood test. On the day of my appointment, I was filled with hope. I needed to know what was going on and I needed confirmation that I was not crazy. When I walked through the door at the doctor's office, Dr. Berman's first words to me were; "You mean no one was able to see just how sick you are?" From the blood work, Dr. Berman determined that I had Graves Disease. Graves Disease is an Autoimmune Disease the leads to overactivity of the thyroid. The next test was a thyroid scan. This test confirmed the Graves Disease. The large lump in my neck was a goiter, which is a swelling in the thyroid gland. Goiters usually occur when the thyroid gland is not functioning properly. The goiter in my neck was considered toxic. The first treatment Dr. Berman wanted to try was Radioactive Iodine. The Radioactive Iodine is absorbed by the thyroid gland and destroys it. I went for several treatments and it was not destroying the thyroid gland. The next option was to remove my thyroid (Thyroidectomy).

    Dr. Berman wanted to do the surgery right away because he feared that my health was severely declining and I could go into a thyroid storm. Thyroid storm is a life-threatening condition that develops in cases of untreated hyperthyroidism. Unfortunately, another problem arose that delayed surgery. I had developed Tachycardia, which is when the heart rate exceeds the normal range for a resting heart rate. The surgery needed to be postponed for 2 weeks while I was put on heart medication to get my heart rate stable. Through all of this, my biggest supporter was Esau. Even though he was scared, he encouraged me to be strong. The night before the surgery, I was surprisingly calm. Dr. Berman was an excellent doctor and very good at explaining what I should expect. I remember Dr.

Berman speaking with me as they were giving me drugs to put me to sleep. The next thing I remember is waking up with a lot of pain in my throat. It was extremely difficult to swallow, and I had a drainage tube coming out of my throat. I survived once again, yet I still did not realize just how blessed I was. Dr. Berman told me that the goiter was the size of a small apple. For a few days, I was not able to eat solid foods. My thyroid was completely removed and that meant I would have to take a pill for the rest of my life. Through all of this, I was able to graduate with honors. My depression got worse. And, yes… I had finally put a label on what I was feeling and it was called, "Depression." No doctors needed to tell me that I was severely depressed. My husband started to notice that things were not right with me. He would question me and I would tell him that nothing was wrong, but after seven years of marriage, he knew me pretty well. My husband was the only person I could attempt to share some of my inner-most feelings. I tried to make him understand how I felt when he told me how beautiful I was. I also tried to make him understand how I viewed my image in the mirror. I told him that I just didn't like what was looking back at me. I could not explain these feelings. We spent hours late at night lying in bed and just talking. I finally felt like there was someone I could share my feelings with and hope for some understanding. He tried to make me understand just how beautiful I was and just how much I had to offer.

CHAPTER 8

The following year after my thyroid surgery, I underwent another surgery. I had a hysterectomy. My doctor recommended a hysterectomy because of severe bleeding and menstrual cycles that lasted 10 to 12 days. There were other problems such as a tilted uterus and my doctor thought the best solution would be the surgery. At this point, I started to feel like the hospital had become my second home. A year after my hysterectomy, I developed a lump under my arm the size of a golf ball. It turned out to be a sebaceous cyst and need to be removed. Fortunately, this was a same day procedure and did not require me to be put to sleep. Will I finally get a break?

It was so very hard for me to develop any type of self-esteem if I am constantly dealing with medical problems. It was at this time I felt like God had some ultimate plan for me. I had a sort of spiritual awakening. I started reading the bible more. I went out and bought a plain English bible because I had difficulty understanding the King James Version. I didn't start going to church but I felt closer to God by reading the bible. I was searching for something and I wasn't quite sure what it was.

Also around this time, I started getting severe headaches. Great! Now I had to deal with migraines. Of course, this was just an assumption. The headaches were followed by numbness when I held my arms up for a short period. It became difficult to do my hair because that required the lifting up of my arms. It was time for a doctor's appointment. I was sent to take a CAT scan. The doctors said the CAT scan came back fine and I was probably experiencing migraine headaches.

I was prescribed Immetrix injections and experienced a severe reaction. At this point, I decided it was time for me to look for a new primary care doctor. That was when I was referred to and met Dr. Catherine O'Neill, who has been my doctor for approximately 15 years. The one quality of Dr. O'Neill that I admire is she was never scared to say she doesn't know and consult with another expert.

As for the headaches, she decided to send me

to a neurosurgeon. Dr. Robert Plunkett was the neurosurgeon I saw, and he first wanted me to take an MRI. He explained that a MRI will show things that a CAT scan will not. After I took the MRI, I got a call from Dr. Plunkett's office that he needed to see me. I was not overly concerned because I didn't expect them to find anything of significance. Well to my surprise, I was about to go through an overwhelming experience. I was told that I had an Arnold Chiari Malformation.

    He might as well have been speaking a foreign language because I had no clue what he was talking about. Arnold Chiari is a malformation of the brain. It is a downward displacement of the cerebellar tonsils through the foramen magnum. The foramen magnum is the opening at the base of the skull that leads to the spinal column. This malformation blocks the flow of spinal fluid. The blockage of spinal fluid also could cause a syrinx to form, eventually leading to syringomyelia. Some symptoms include hand weakness, dissociated sensory loss and in severe cases, paralysis could occur. Dr. Plunkett suggested surgery, brain surgery. Decompression surgery was the treatment recommended.

    Decompression surgery is when the lamina of the first and sometimes the second or even third cervical vertebrae and part of the occipital bone of the skull is removed to relieve pressure and allow the normal flow of spinal fluid. My question was what happens if I do not go forward with this surgery? Dr. Plunkett was very honest with me and stated that there was a very real probability that I would experience paralysis from the waist up. The numbness I experienced when raising my arms would not go away (permanent damage) but it would not get worse if I proceeded with the surgery. The thought of being partially paralyzed was enough for me to decide to move forward with the surgery. I had many questions but the first question was did my head have to get shaved. He said the back and sides would need to be shaved. I thought why not have the whole head instead of leaving a patch of hair on the top. He scheduled the surgery for two weeks later to give me time to talk with my family and for them absorb what was about to take place. My recovery time would be approximately 6 months. There was a possibility it could be longer.

During this time, I started to pray. Maybe I should say it was the time that I started to have serious conversations with God. Surprisingly, I did not beg for mercy. My prayers were about God's will. I had to come to the realization that I needed to have faith in God and not question his will. I prayed for comfort and understanding for my family. This was a major surgery, and I honestly was not afraid or apprehensive. I always believed that when your time comes to die, there is nothing you can do about it. You should just make sure you live every day trying to be the best person you can be. If I didn't make it through this surgery, it was just my time and I was ok with that. If I made it through this surgery that means God feels that I have more work to do.

It was hard for Esau and he found it difficult to understand how I could be so calm before the surgery. He threw a party for me, with some of my closest friends, a week before the surgery. He tried everything possible to be supportive and help me not worry. I talked with my children the night before the surgery and they seemed calm and understanding.

The morning of the surgery, Dr. Plunkett explained what would happen during the surgery. He explained that screws would be inserted on the sides of my head to secure a surgical halo. The incision would be from the top back of my head all the way down my neck. Once the surgery was complete, I would be moved from the operating room to the intensive care unit, until I became stable enough to be moved to a room. As he was talking to me the anesthesiologist was injecting anesthesia into my IV and the next thing I recall was waking up in ICU with a severe headache.

Severe doesn't even begin to describe the pain that I was feeling.

I did not know that a person's head could hurt so badly. The doctor ordered a morphine drip. This helped a little with the pain but I only had peace when I was asleep. I didn't take a look at myself in the mirror for several days due to the severe pain. But when finally took a look at myself, all I could do was cry. After having your head cut open I didn't expect to look like a queen, but for some reason, all the ugliness I have tried to escape came flooding back. All I wanted was to live my life and feel good about myself.

CHAPTER 9

The recovery process went well but emotionally I was spiraling downward. I shaved the small patch of hair on the top of my head and was completely bald. I couldn't wear a wig just yet because of the bandages. During this time, I very seldom left my bedroom. I only left my bedroom to go to the bathroom and to go to a doctor's appointment. Dr. Plunkett was extremely pleased and surprised at how quickly I was recovering. I sunk into the deepest depression of my life at this point. During the day when my husband was at work, I spent the day watching television and crying. Many afternoons, Esau would come home and find me crying for no explainable reason. I would look in the mirror and see a person so unhappy with herself. I loved to read, and I did a lot of reading. When I read, I escaped. I left reality and immersed myself in the books I was reading. This was my answer to not dealing with my problems. I would get upset if anyone interrupted my reading. It felt good to become a character in a book. It was as if I could create a person who had everything that I was missing.

The other girl's journey: The other girl was a beautiful girl and had an almost perfect existence. She had a family that thought she was the best and friends who dreamed of being like her. The other girl traveled to many places and was well educated. When she looked in the mirror she smiled, never did she cry. She saw an image that inspired her. She saw a beautiful person. The other girl existed in my head and I needed her journey to fill the void in my life. I needed to live through her in order to forget about the image I saw in the mirror. I wanted to see the same image that the other girl saw. There were times I looked in the mirror and saw a beautiful image but in my head, I was quickly reminded that I was only seeing what I wanted to see and the truth was that image was not pretty. It wasn't all about vanity because it was truly deeper than that. I just wanted to feel comfortable around people and not second guess people. I didn't want to play out my life in my head; I wanted to experience life. There was a part of me that knew I had to leave my world of make-believe and return to reality.

My husband was just the right person to bring me back to reality to face my problems. Esau came home from work one evening and lit a fire under me. When he walked through the door, he could see I had just finished crying. In a stern voice, he said, "What is your problem? You are sitting here crying and feeling sorry for yourself. You are an intelligent and educated woman and you could get any job you want if you put your mind to it. Get off your ass and get your shit together." I got so pissed off and how dare he speak to me this way. I later learned from Esau that this was a last ditch effort to get me out of the house and back to living again. The following day I went to a wig shop and purchased a wig and made an appointment with an employment agency. It only took me two weeks before I was working again but was I truly living again? After working for six months, my hair started to grow back, and I was able to stop wearing the wigs. I started to confide in Esau more about my feelings. He found it difficult to understand why I felt the way I did. He often told me how beautiful I was and always tried to encourage me. I thought about seeing a psychiatrist again but I was very hesitant. But I decide to talk with Dr. O'Neill once again and see if she could make a recommendation. Once again, I just flirted with the notion of seeking professional help. There was something inside of me that said I and only I could win this battle. The most important thing I later discovered is that will only happen with the help of God.

CHAPTER 10

My turning point came after my brain surgery. I thought about the fact that I was letting an image in the mirror control and dictate who I was. I started thinking, and I finally realized that there had to be a reason for my survival. If I could transform my life and take what I have learned and share it, and if only one person benefits from my experiences, then my job is done. Over the years after my brain surgery, I began to realize just how strong I was and what things matter most in life. What you do in life affects the physical beauty that people see. There was no magic pill or extensive therapy that helped me realize my potential; it was faith, determination and courage. I wanted to change; I needed to change and so I changed.

I began to feel an intense need to go to

church. I wanted to have a closer relationship with God. I wanted to hand all my problems over to him. I have always had faith in God, but it was now time for me to learn his word and to live my life according to his word. It was now time for me to accept Christ into my life. Esau and I took that journey together, but for me, the true healing process was beginning. The only way to explain it is to say it was a rebirth. I felt like I was starting my life from the beginning. I had to learn to trust God.

Today, I live every day to the fullest. I keep God first in my life and try to live my life accordingly. I no longer worry about what people think of me. I try to inspire and uplift people and hope that my experiences will help someone find the courage needed to cope with those dark moments in their lives. I find myself praying quite often. I actually believe in my heart that God hears our prayers. But what I did not understand was why some of my prayers went unanswered. At least I thought they were not answered. What I learned is that what God has in store for you may not be the same thing you are seeking. Yes, God answers prayers but he also knows what is best for you. With that being said, there are times we pray for things that are not good for us. Those are the prayers we think go unanswered. When I think about the things I have prayed for, I realized that God truly does answer prayers. I have prayed for deliverance from the image in the mirror and I have finally learned how to listen to God. The answer has always been within me. I have learned that I do not need anyone to tell me how beautiful I am because I am filled with the spirit of God and I have such a renewed spirit. The image in the mirror is no longer important. I find myself often thinking of the lyrics to a song Bishop Paul Morton sang:

> *Your tears are just temporary relief.*
> *Your tears are just a release of the pain, sorrow,*
> *grief.*
> *Your tears are expressions that can't be*
> *controlled.*
> *A little crying out is alright,*
> *But after a while you won't have to cry*
> *no more;*
> *Don't you worry, God's gonna wipe every*
> *tear away.*
> *Weeping may endure for a night,*
> *Joy will come in the morning.*
> *Hold on to his unchanging hand,*
> *Brand new day is to come.*

I now know that it is alright to cry because

tomorrow brings a new day. I have taken a journey recently that has allowed me to have a better understanding of myself. This has been a time of discovery. My journey has been a new and personal relationship with God. A spiritual awakening that has allowed me to see something totally different when I look into the mirror. I don't see an ugly portrait any longer; I see a beautiful person because my heart is laced with the love of God.

CHAPTER 11

Romeo Vitelli, Ph.D. states:

> One of the greatest traumas imaginable is when parents have to deal with the death of a child. Producing greater stress than dealing with the death of a parent or spouse, a child's death is especially traumatic because it is often unexpected as well as being in violation of the usual order of things in which the child is expected to bury the parent. The emotional blow associated with child loss can lead to a wide range of psychological and physiological

problems including depression, anxiety, cognitive and physical symptoms linked to stress, marital problems, increased risk for suicide, pain and guilt. All of these issues can persist long after the child's death and may lead to diagnosed psychiatric conditions such as complicated grief disorder (currently under review for inclusion in the DSM-5), which can include many symptoms similar to post-traumatic stress disorder.

How do you come back? Is your life forever changed? Where do you draw strength? These are just a few of the questions that arise out of the tragedy of parents losing their children. Before October 4, 2013, I could only imagine how a parent might feel. Even trying to imagine was difficult. As a mother, you carry a child for nine months and you never give a thought of losing that child. Journey with me as I discover how to go on living in spite of the tragedy.

CHAPTER 12

I only have two vivid memories of my father. I was at the kitchen table and I would not eat my vegetables. My father was coming into the kitchen and I went to duck under the kitchen table and busted my lip. Today I still have the scar right above my lip. The other memory was my father lying in his coffin. That was my introduction to death at the age of 4 years old. Of course at the age of 4, I really didn't comprehend the dark side of death. I am sure I missed my dad, but I went on to do the things little girls do. I did not become depressed, or have a mental breakdown. I just went on and adjusted. I really did not recognize the impact of the death of my father until I was a teenager. There was no grieving process but as I grew older, there was the longing to know what it would be like to have a father. I didn't start wondering what it would be like to have a father until my teenage years. I was not grieving the loss of my father as much as I was missing what I did not have.

It is funny how things happen in your life and understanding may not come for years. You don't think twice about certain situations. You just experience life and understanding comes later. I was raised with my sister by my grandmother (my father's mother).

My grandmother had four children; my father; Matthew, his twin sister; Martha, Logie (Harris) and Helena. My father's twin sister died as an infant and I never got the facts about her death. My father died when he was 24 years old. My grandmother had lost three of her four children. I have no memory of her hurt or pain after losing two children. One evening I was sitting in the bedroom with my grandmother and she got a phone call. She dropped the phone and let out a heart-wrenching scream. I was eighteen years old at this time and I had never seen my grandmother scream the way she did this day. Her third child was killed in a trucking accident. My uncle was killed, and I was sad but I had no understanding of what my grandmother was feeling. It was another death of a loved one. Nothing different for me but I could not have imagined. My grandmother did not talk about her pain. Today I wondered how she did it. How did she find the strength to move on? Where did she draw her strength? There are so many questions I would have like to have asked her but at that time I had no understanding. She gave birth to four children and only had one living child. I can only imagine the depths of her pain. One part of me wishes I could have asked my grandmother questions about her feelings but I now know nothing can prepare you.

No one else's experiences can help you with your own experiences. Experience means living it out for yourself. Never during that time did I think about mom losing her children. My thought process was my uncle has died. No depth to that. My thoughts took me back to other people in my life that have lost a child and at those times there was no understanding. I am sure I said the standard, "I am sorry for your loss", "I can only imagine how you must feel", etc. Statements I wish I could take back. I now know not saying anything is sometimes best.

As a young child, I did not tend to form strong relationships with family members. My sister, on the other hand, was good at forming and making those necessary connections with all family members near and far. I established those strong bonds with the immediate family. Often my sister would say, "Do you remember so and so?", and I honestly had no clue. Not sure of why I was that way, but I was content with the distance. And it was not because of a lack of love. Being that way also provided a cushion for when death came along. Today, I actually long for those close relationships. Death seen through the lens of a child seems different. Loving relationships seen through the lens of a child seems different. There are so many things that we don't know as a child and it allows us to experience things differently than adults. Adults have so many life experiences and knowledge that allows them to experience life situations in a different way. We know that no one lives forever but when that time comes we are still heartbroken because nothing can truly prepare you to say goodbye to a loved one. We not only miss that physical person but we miss the memories and the impact that they have on your life.

CHAPTER 13

If someone told me that I would be married with three children, I would have argued that fact. Fact is, I had always dreamed of being a single businesswoman traveling the world. I never had a desire to have children. It was not in my game plan. Well, I learned later in life that God's plans for our lives don't always line up with our plans. I had to readjust my whole game plan and goals. Today, I realized that it has been a journey of seeking out my purpose and until I surrendered all to Christ, it would not be clear what my purpose was to be. I am learning to appreciate my struggles in life as much as my successes. It is those struggles that make me the person I am today. Of course, when you have to change your life plans, the journey has some bumps along the way.

After I graduated high school, I thought I met the man of my dreams. The reality was he did not have the same feelings for me. I ended up pregnant with my first child at the age of twenty-one and unmarried. His immediate answer to what he referred to as a problem was to get an abortion. Abortion was the furthest thing from my mind and I was determined to have this child with or without him. It was without him. My grandmother was my rock during this time. When I went into labor, it was my grandmother who called the ambulance and rode with me to the hospital. It was my grandmother who held my hand during the labor pains. I gave birth to my first child; eight pounds and 4 ounces and I had a son. Derek was my world and at that time being my only child, my grandmother spoiled him rotten. This was her first great-grandchild, and he meant the world to her. After I had Derek, I decided to go to college and try to get a degree but I was not ready and I dropped out of college. That is when I met the love of my life. He loves telling the story of how we met on a Wednesday, moved in on Friday and proposed marriage on Saturday. Well, many thought I was crazy but I am thankful for my husband of thirty years. When I met my husband, Derek was eighteen months old. I went on to have two more sons (actually trying for that girl) and even though they were not in my game plan; I am so thankful to God for my husband and children. There was no handbook that helped with being a wife and mother. It was on-the-job training at its core.

I was not prepared for the struggles we would face as a family. I had to learn that it was no longer about me but that it was about us. My sister and I were raised by my grandmother and we were taught how to be strong and independent women. So it was an adjustment for me to follow my husband when I was used to being a leader. There were many lessons to come during thirty years of marriage. The biggest lesson was how to be the best mother you could be!! There is always the thought of what else could I have done? How else could I have shown my love? Through all the joys of being a wife and mother, there were plenty of growing pains and learning experiences.

November 9, 1986, I woke up tired of being pregnant. It looked like this baby had no intentions on coming into the world. One and a half weeks overdue and I was tired of carrying this load. A friend had told me about drinking castor oil to induce labor. And there I sat with a bottle of castor oil in front of me contemplating drinking it. I was already two centimeters dilated but nothing was happening. I asked for my husband's input and he basically said whatever you want to do is ok with me as long as it is safe. He provided a safe answer. Don't get me wrong because this was my second child, and I did enjoy being pregnant, but nine months is all a girl can take. So I got some ginger ale and mixed the small bottle of castor oil with the ginger ale and drank it.

A few hours later I am in the delivery room and it seems like there were no breaks between contractions. I remember the doctor telling me not to push yet but I had an intense urge to push. Not long after, I gave birth to a healthy baby boy that weighed eight pounds and two ounces. We named him Brian Matthew Spruill. He was my second child of three boys. I always wanted girls, but I grew to love the attention a mom gets from her sons. Out of all three of my sons, Brian was the momma's boy, even though they all had a little of the momma's boy in them.

Even though I wanted a girl, my husband agreed our family was complete with two boys. Well, God has a way of showing you that what you want does not always line up with his will. I was going for a routine GYN appointment and I took a urine and blood test. I was sitting in the room waiting for the doctor and the nurse stuck her head in and said: "did you know that you were pregnant?" April 27th, 1990, I gave birth to Patrick James Spruill, my third son. Derek, Brian and Patrick, my children and my family was complete.

After the birth of my children, I never imagined or entertained the thought of losing them. I have heard of other parents that have lost their children for one reason or another, but I still never let such thoughts creep into my mind. When hearing of a parent losing their child, it went through my mind as any other death would. Not to mention unexpected death. Unexpected death is like having your breath snatched from you and not being able to breathe. Never getting the chance to say goodbye or I love you. You just don't think about it until it happens to you. If I heard about someone who died unexpectedly once again it just went through my mind as any other death would. It never dawned on me how impactful the unexpected loss of a child could be.

CHAPTER 14

Brian had an infectious smile and passion for life. As a small child, Brian seemed reserved at home. We actually thought Brian was quiet and shy. Well, we soon found out that he was not that quiet. We received many reports from school and they all basically said the same thing: "Brian is very intelligent, but he talks too much". Our shy son was not as shy as we thought he was. He always made the honor roll but could not stop talking. His teachers stated that he had to be the center of attention in the classroom. His father decided to take a surprise trip to school and there he was cracking jokes when everyone was supposed to be quietly doing their work. Well, his father left a lasting impression. He often told his friends that story.

Through all his clowning around in school, he was always a straight-A student.

The first time I felt helpless as a mother was when Brian broke his femur bone. He was playing with his brother running into his room and as he went to jump in the bed, he hit his leg on the metal frame of the bed. The bone in his thigh was protruding but had not broken through the skin. My husband held the bone down while I called the ambulance. The EMT said that my husband holding down the bone actually saved his life. He was 4 years old. When we got to the hospital, the doctors examined him and told us that he had broken his femur bone. Watching my baby lying in that hospital bed crying in pain and not being able to comfort him was so emotionally painful. He ended up in a full body cast. This was an especially difficult time for me because I was also pregnant with my youngest son. These are the tough moments that you can't prepare for as a parent. Your maternal instinct just kicks in and you find the best way to love and care for your children. I did not want to leave his side while he was in the hospital. My husband and I took turns staying overnight at the hospital. With a full body cast on, it was just like having a baby all over again. We had to put diapers on him and he was pretty much immobile. When the cast was removed, he was in a wheelchair and he had to learn how to walk all over again. It was not easy, but we didn't complain, we kicked into overdrive and did what we had to do to make sure our children were taken care of. This was the natural order of things. Once Brian healed and was walking again, there were no lingering effects. Although Brian would often joke that he was lopsided now because one leg was shorter than the other.

As Brian grew into an adult, he discovered he had a passion for fashion design. He went to college for a short stint but college was not for him. I was ok with that as long as he did something productive, like work. I knew Brian would be successful because he was driven and had determination. Not to mention he was extremely stubborn and selfish at times. I was that parent who did not take a blind eye to my child's faults. When I was critiquing them I was honest. This was the only way to get them to recognize their shortcomings. Brian came to me one day and told me that he wanted to become a fashion designer. Well in the back of my mind, I thought why not a lawyer, Doctor or some other profession, but as a mother, I encouraged him to pursue his dreams. And that is exactly what he did. He wrote a few articles for some fashion magazines and did several photos-shoots in New York, San Diego, Toronto and

Chicago. He was beginning to live his dream, and this is what I admired that about Brian.

I often say I have a cheerleading team because my husband and my sons supported everything I did. Brian had a knack for cheering his mom on and always had an encouraging word. There was nothing that I could do wrong in his eyes.

CHAPTER 15

Thursday night, October 3, 2013, was an ordinary work night. I went to bed around 11:30 pm and slept soundly until 5:30 am when my husband's phone rang. He did not answer it and then my phone rang. When I looked at my phone, I realized that I had three missed calls from this same phone number. There was an unknown panic rising in the pit of my stomach. I answered the phone and the woman's voice on the other end asked: "Are you the mother of Brian Spruill?" I said yes, and she said: "You need to come to South Buffalo Mercy Hospital right away". I then asked, "What was wrong?" She responded, "You just need to get here right away". At that moment that sinking feeling in the pit of my stomach became real. My husband and I got dressed in silence and drove to the hospital in total silence. Anyone who knew my husband, and I know we are never silent when we are in the car together. We dared not speak what was lying on our hearts. I believe we were thinking about what lied ahead of us. I think so many scenarios ran through my head. I just did not want to think about what I knew in my heart.

We arrived at the hospital and went to the security desk for directions to the emergency room. I don't know if it was just me but the hospital lobby had an eerie and gloomy presence. The security guard walked us back to the emergency room. The woman behind the desk told the security guard she needed to walk us back to receiving room A. Walking down that corridor was the longest walk of my life and it seemed like the hallway would never end. As she was taking us into the room, my husband asked: "what about our son?" She stated she needed to get the doctor to talk with us. As we entered the room, the first thing I notice was a pamphlet on the table with a candle on it and the pamphlet was for grief counseling. I knew but refused to know.

The doctor came in with a nurse and sat down. She was a young pregnant doctor. How ironic that she was about to bring life into this world. She said, "Your son, Brian was in a serious car accident and he was not wearing a seat belt. He was a passenger, and it seems the driver might have been speeding and they crashed into a cement utility pole." My husband said, "Well what about our son?" And she said, "I am sorry but he did not make it." "I sorry but he did not make it", "I am sorry, but he did not make it". I just kept hearing that over and over again in my head trying to process what I was hearing. My world stood still and my life completely changed at that moment. Today I still can't explain the range of emotions I felt at that moment. In my mind, I thought about God not giving you more than you could bear. I had changed my life, and I was serving God. I was not perfect, but I definitely made changes for the better. Through the initial pain, I wanted to trust God, but I was struggling. How do I make it back from this? Do I make it back from this? Where do I go from here?

My husband and I were left in the room to try to process this before going to see Brian. I was not able to process anything at that moment because I just kept hearing that doctor say he did not make it. It was like a record that kept skipping and repeating. I thought this was the beginning of me losing my mind. I have overcome so much, but I was not sure that I could come back from this. I lost my mother in 2010 and that was difficult, but the pain I felt from that loss did not compare.

As we went to see Brian, I had this sick hope that he was not dead and I would walk in that room and see my son smiling at me. As I walked through that door, I felt a rush of anxiety overtake me. He looked like he was sleeping. I wanted to say "Brian wake up now!!" My Brian was not waking up. I walked over and touched his hand; so cold. I touched his face; so cold. My baby was not waking up. He looked peaceful. He had a neck brace on and the only visual sign of injuries was a small gash on his forehead. We stayed at the hospital for more than 5 hours. Family and friends came together and prayed. I met so many of his friends. They just kept coming. Seeing him laying on that hospital gurney was so unreal. I was not able to process this in my mind. I felt the pain, but it just did not feel real. I just wanted Brian to get up and say something. It was almost noon and time for us to leave the hospital because they needed to transport him the county medical examiner. The drive home was so surreal. I still kept relieving that moment when the doctor said: "he did not make it". I don't think I will ever be able to get that out of my head. I was still unable to process the events that took place. I struggled to understand why this was happening to me. I trust and believe in God but at that moment I was angry and could not understand how God could allow this to happen. The anger was building and yes I started questioning God and wondering why God would allow this to happen. Was this my reward for committing to God? I was in the habit of praying daily but this day, I could not pray. Anger kept me from talking to God. When we gathered in the room where Brian was to pray, my mind was wandering not praying. My mind and thought process were blurred. I needed to be busy. I kicked into gear, calling the funeral home, the cemetery and a lawyer. Keeping myself busy kept me from feeling or thinking.

The house started filling up with people and this became my distraction. October 4th 2013 after everyone went home, it was just Esau, and I left to absorb what took place. We cried and held each other. Oh, how I welcomed sleep that night. I wanted to sleep so bad because my hope was when I woke up, I would realize that I had a horrible dream.

Wow, I just had a nightmare. I just dreamed that Brian was dead. I can't even repeat what I dreamed about. I just wanted to pick up the phone and call Brian. I dial his number and on the third ring, he answered the phone. I was so glad to talk to my son. Brian, I need to see you today. It was imperative that I saw him as soon as possible because that nightmare had me shook. "Mom, I will stop by after work". I would see my son soon. I went downstairs to tell my husband about my dream and the stair took me into this dark dank dingy basement. When I reached the bottom of the steps, the steps disappeared. I was trapped in this place. I screamed, and no one heard my screams. I needed to get out of here because Brian was coming over after work. I suddenly saw a ghost-like image of Brian. I was speechless and Brian spoke, "Mom I must go". Brian, you can't go! Please do not leave me!! And he faded away, and it got pitch black. Out of the darkness, there were hands coming out and surrounding me and I quickly sat up in bed breathing heavily. I began to cry as I realized that I was dreaming. I felt like my world had come to an end. After that, I found it hard to sleep through the night and I was always awake at 5:30 in the morning. It was as if I had a built-in alarm clock.

I had a doctor's appointment and decided maybe I should talk to my doctor about my feelings and what has been going on. I told him what happened to Brian, but that was all. He said he was concerned about me and he wanted me to see a psychiatrist who specialized in grief counseling. When I left his office, I had every intention to go and see this doctor. I called her and made an appointment and that is as far as I got. I was not ready to express my pain to anyone. Even though she was a grief counselor, would she truly understand the depths of my pain? I just wanted to be left alone so I could ignore what I was feeling. For the first time in four years I thought about smoking a cigarette and for the first time in many years, I thought about having a drink. My logic was so off because I felt like no matter how you try to live life correctly, you can't avoid the heartache that life brings. But I knew better because I was just looking for a reason to drink and smoke. It was just a thought because deep in my heart I wanted to do what was pleasing in the sight of God. It always came back to God. Through the heartache, it always came back to God. Through the hurt and pain, it was God who I still wanted to please. Not fully trusting him right at that moment, I still had a need to please Him.

My oldest son, Derek put together a benefit for Brian before his funeral. The benefit was beautiful and so many people came out. The mayor was there and local news media was also there. It was wonderful to meet so many of his friends and church family. It was a time of reflection and remembrance. The place where this was held had a balcony, and I found a moment alone to go out on the balcony and reflect on my feelings. I needed to believe that I would be alright. I got the chance to have a conversation with one of Brian's friends, Lauren and she told me about an incident that occurred the day before the accident. Brian, Lauren and another co-worker were driving to get lunch. As Lauren was driving, a woman cut her off and Brian was very upset. She asked Brian why he was so upset and he stated: "I have a fear of dying in a car accident". How ironic that a day later he died in a car accident.

CHAPTER 16

*B*efore I could go to sleep that second night after Brian's death, I needed to know why God would allow this to happen. I needed to search his Word and find some type of understanding and meaning to this tragedy. And most of all why me?

Psalm 34: *The Lord is nigh unto them that are of a broken heart; and saveth such as be of a contrite spirit.* There were so many scriptures about God providing comfort, but nothing about why God would allow you to go through such pain. In my heart, I knew, but the pain prevented me from realizing what I already knew. I continued to search the scriptures for answers. Until this one scripture resonated within me and I began to see things differently. Isaiah 43:2 *When thou most passe through the waters, I will be with thee; and through the rivers, they shall not overflow thee; when thou wouldst through the fire, thou shalt not be burned; neither shall the flame kindle upon thee.* God never promised that we would not endure trials, but he did promise that he would be there with us to be a comforter. Then I thought of another bible verse I knew so well. John 3:16 *For God so loved the world, that he gave his only begotten Son, that whosoever Blyth in him should not perish, but have everlasting life.* God himself knew what it meant to lose a child as He witnessed the crucifixion of his His Son Jesus on the cross. These revelations did not erase the pain, but I was able to let go of some of my anger for now.

When I woke the following morning, all I could do was cry and finally, I was able to pray. I asked God to send his Holy Spirit to comfort me because I did not have the strength to deal with this. I needed to lean fully on God. I knew that my faith in God was the only thing to see me through this tragedy. My anger became redirect at the young lady driving the car that night and the other two passengers. They all survived.

There were four people in the car that morning and the only one who died was my son. I needed someone to blame and a new anger arose within me. I was not angry with God any longer but I was angry with the young lady driving the car. I just wanted my son to have a chance at life and I felt she was responsible for taking that chance away. Was she speeding, was she drunk, what were the circumstances around the accident. I was instructed by my lawyer not to contact the young lady because it was now a legal matter and they would contact her going forward. I was so angry because none of the passengers in the car reached out to my husband or me. All I could think about is if that was me, I would want the parents to know that I was sorry. Not a word from the driver or other passengers. What were they thinking? Were they sorry or did they not even care? Once again, I took these feelings to God in prayer. I did not want the anger to fester. I needed to keep God front and center in my life at this time if I were to have any chance of surviving this and I honestly did not know any other way to get through this. There was speculation that she was speeding and it was raining that night. These details helped fuel the anger. But there was the Holy Spirit speaking to me telling me to forgive. I was not ready to forgive, and I needed that anger at that moment. The anger also helped me to cope and deal with Brian's death.

    I started searching Brian's Facebook pictures to see if I can find this young lady. I found one picture of her with Brian and another friend. It felt like I stared at that picture for an eternity. I thought if I saw her face, I would find answers. At that point, I began to pray. I needed to forgive this young lady because this was Brian's friend and she did not get behind the wheel of that car intending to kill Brian. But I was not ready to forgive because there was some sort of comfort in that anger and being able to have someone to blame. I put aside my feelings for a brief moment and imagined what she must be feeling. And at that moment I wanted to forgive her, but I still struggled. To this day, I have not met or seen the young lady, but my prayer is that she will find peace. I do wish that I will have an opportunity to meet her and let her know that I don't blame here. I want that opportunity because she is the one who spent the last moments of Brian's life with him. I am hoping she can share those moments with me.

I understand how it feels when you think you are losing your mind. I understand how it would be easy to turn to suicide. I understand how you might want to sink into a never-ending depression. It is so hard to get lost during a time like this. I suffer from depression and I was aware of where this could take me. I was trying to get myself ready for the biggest fight of my life and I accomplished this by realizing it was not my fight to have. I did not want to sink into depression because I know how hard that can be and this time I was not sure if I would be able to find my way back. I started having those feelings of impending doom and anxiety set in. I strapped in for this roller coaster ride of emotions. I started researching grief following the loss of a child. I came across one article about a couple in the UK. Their nine-year-old son was killed in a crash. But what they did after was sad. Below is an excerpt of the article by Aislan Cramb, Scottish Correspondent:

> They remained by his hospital bedside for six days before they had to take the decision to turn off his life support machine. Weeks later his father Allan, 30, took his own life.
> Kelly Hogg, 31, from Glasgow, who also has a 13-year-old daughter, said their son's death was more than they could bear.
> She added: "Allan took his own life and died happy and content knowing that he was going to see his son again and that he would be there to look after him.
> "It also gave me some comfort that my wee boy was with his daddy, who loved him more than anything in the world, and he wasn't out there all alone.
> "I know it might sound strange to some

> people but when you are about to lose a child you love more than anything in the world, you want to do everything in your power to protect them. If that means taking your own life, then that is the sacrifice we decided to make."

Before Brian died, I might have called these parents crazy, but I learned that grief can affect everyone differently. The loss of a child can cause people to lose what sanity they have. But by the grace of God that could have been me. That was not the answer, but I was oh so familiar with the pain. I found another interesting article by Carrie Dann, ABC News Medical Unit:

> When her 19-year-old daughter, Amanda, died in a car accident in 1993, Susan Gilbert said her grief was exhausting. "I didn't sleep for a year. I slept for maybe half an hour a night," she said. "The experience is really beyond words."
> Today, Gilbert works with other parents whose children have died, and said the loss affects all aspects of their lives. "

> While you do learn to live with it, you don't get over it," she said.
>
> New research suggests that such parents can suffer devastating, long-lasting health consequences as a result of the death.

The articles made me pause and think. As tragic as these stories were, something was missing. I do not know if any of these parents had a relationship with God, but I did know that there was a difference in these two stories. The first story of the couple seemed like hope was missing. The second story provided some hope. Susan Gilbert was so right when she said, "While you do learn to live with it, you don't get over it". I don't think I will ever get over the death of my son, but I am learning how to continue living and keep his memory alive. I don't want a feeling of hopelessness. I would first have to bury my son and then focus on what's next. In my heart, I knew it would be nobody but God who would see me through.

CHAPTER 17

The first week after Brian's death was the hardest. My husband was concerned about our youngest son, Patrick. He could not understand why he did not cry and he did not seem sad about his brother's death. I explained to my husband that everyone grieves differently and we needed to respect how he was handling this. I decide to talk to Patrick to find out how he was really doing. He said he was fine and believed that Brian was ok because of a dream that he had. He said he woke up and Brian was sitting on the edge of his bed. Brian said he was ok and when he went to reach for him, he disappeared. This gave Patrick comfort. I truly believe that this was the way he was dealing and when he was ready he would have his moment to cry. He was more concerned about how his father and I were doing. He became extremely protective over us during this time.

We did not schedule the funeral until October 14, 2013, in order to allow time for my in-laws to arrive from Atlanta. I thank God for blessing me with a God fearing and praying mother-in-law. Sylvia Cooper provided that extra layer of strength that my husband and I needed. She was our rock during this time. During that week there were two separate worlds for me: day and night. During the day there were people coming and going. Family, my church family, and friends all came and provided support and comfort. With all of the family and friends surrounding us and reminiscing about Brian, I was able to avoid thinking or feeling. Many mistook this for strength. Little did they know I felt so weak and lost. During the night there were feelings and plenty of thinking. I cried some nights and I felt like there was an empty pit that opened up and would not allow me to stop crying. My heart ached like I never knew it could. At this point, I just wanted my son back. I started praying like I never prayed before. I needed God to send me some comfort and I knew that was the only place I could turn. I just wanted the Holy Spirit to wrap his loving arms around me. No one could provide that but God. I believed this in my heart but the pain was real and I did not want to feel the pain any longer.

I was learning so many new things about my son. I learned how he had made an impact on so many people's lives. I met so many of his friends that truly loved him. The friends and family were my comforts during the day and at night I had my husband. We were the only two that truly felt the same hurt. His brothers were in pain, his aunts were in pain, his cousins were in pain and his friends were in pain. Everyone felt pain but no one shared what my husband and I shared; the loss of a child. My pastor, (Pastor James R. Banks) shared something with me that week that I tried to hold on to. He said, "You never stop feeling the pain, you just have to learn to live with it and it was ok to be angry. Just don't stay there". I told my pastor that I wanted to say some words about Brian at the funeral and he told me what better person is there to do the eulogy than you. First thought was, would I be able to hold it together long enough to eulogize my son. At that point I did what I do best; I prayed. So I began writing his eulogy. Another busy activity to help keep me distracted. Some thought it would be difficult for me to write and then read it, but writing it was therapy for me.

The Eulogy

TRIBULATION TO VICTORY: BIRTH OF A QUEEN

To you, O Lord, we humbly entrust Brian, so precious in your sight. Take him into your arms and welcome him into paradise, where there will be no sorrow, no weeping nor pain, but the fullness of peace and joy with Your Son and the Holy Spirit forever ever. Amen.

At the end of every day, as he rests from his labors, every man asks himself, "Have I made my mom and dad proud? Did I make their worlds at least a little bit better?" Ever a caring son, this is the way that Brian Matthew Spruill lived his life.

Brian was born in Brooklyn, New York and although he spent the majority of his life in Buffalo, he had a great love for New York City. Brian excelled in school and was an honor student all the way through school. He loved to talk. Only reports from school were Brian talks too much.

Brian was the middle child and at times he wanted to be the youngest and other times he acted like the oldest. As brothers do they argued but at the end of the day, they loved and protected each other. Patrick would come to me or his father for advice but he had to call Brian to verify our responses. Derek stepped in as Brian second father figure but everyone that knew Brian knows how that turned out.

My husband Esau, loves his boys. I would worry about him being so strict on them but many times Brian would tell me, as a grown adult, that he appreciated this because it made him understand how much he loved his dad and how much his dad loved him. Esau affectionately nicknamed him B-lo. They did not always see eye to eye (Brian liked the Lakers and my husband liked the Knicks) but there was always love and respect.

Cookie, Marissa and Helena, his aunts and cousin. In this case, cousin equals sister because Marissa was Brian's baby sister. Brian loved both Helena and Cookie and this was our immediate little circle.

Atlanta, GA. Do you think Brian waited for a family trip to go and spend time with Grandma Sylvia? He loved his grandma Sylvia and his aunts, Shelly, Dionne, Daisy and his uncle Frank. He had planned to spend his first Thanksgiving ever in Atlanta with Grandma this year.

There is not enough time in this day to talk about all the friends he had but there are four specials friends I grew to love as my other children, Eric, Sharelle, Chris and Kenyon.

One of my husband's and my greatest joys is my son got to know the Lord before he passed. I want to thank Bishop Alvarez and The Way family for embracing my son. He truly loved the Lord.

Anyone who knew Brian knew he had a contagious smile and just wanted to live life. When Brian came to me and said mom I really want to be a fashion stylist and he was very passionate about this, I thought maybe this was a phase. But we all knew how he lived this dream. He made it happen. He did several photos shoots in New York, Chicago, San Diego and Toronto. He started a fashion blog and wrote several articles for some fashion magazines. He always talked about fashion week in New York City and just recently he went to New York City for fashion

> week. I admired how he lived his dream. I think if each and every one of you could tell me something amazing about Brian, I would have more than enough to write a novel.
>
> Many friends and family have expressed their sympathies but I had to remind myself that Brian belongs to the Lord and he allowed us 26 years to experience loving Brian. So as hard as it is, let us celebrate Brian in the grand way that my son would expect. Thank you, Jesus, for all that you have done, all that you are doing and all that you will do.

We went to the funeral home to view the body. This was a private viewing for the immediate family. This was the first time I would see Brian since seeing him at the hospital. As I walked in the room, I just lost control and let out a cry that needed to be released. My mother-in-law, Sylvia started praying. I was able to pull myself together and there I stood looking at my son as if he was just sleeping.

Sunday, October 6th, God sent me a little comfort. My friend Sonia has a grandson name, Rodney. We call him little Rodney. He was 2 years old at this time and not known to go to you very easily. The most I could get out of him was hello. We all sit together during morning worship service. Well, this particular morning he was playing with his cars and all of sudden he jumped up in my lap. Of course, I was surprised but what happened next is what had me speechless. He took his two little hands and held my face and began kissing me. He would kiss me and then lay his head on my chest and then he started kissing me again and this went on for about 15 minutes. He then jumped down and began playing with his car again. It was not until the next day that I realized what happened. I did not cry that night. I felt at peace. I woke up feeling the same way and when I realized what just happened, all I could do is say "Thank you, Lord!!!" Little Rodney was the comfort that I had been praying for. Did comfort mean all was well and I would not feel any more pain? The answer is no and honestly, this was the beginning of a lifelong journey for me.

Monday, October 14th, 2013 – This was the day I would say goodbye to Brian. I promised that I was going to be strong. My family gathered at the house and we got dressed to go to the church. I wore white and husband wore a grey suit. We busied ourselves getting ready. The limousine arrived and we were on our way. I was going to be fine. When we arrived at the church, there was already a crowd forming. As we entered the church, Patrick finally cried and broke down. His brother Derek was there to support him. Walking down the aisle of the church was one of the longest walks of my life. The closer I got to the coffin, the more I started to realize this was going to be the last time I would see my son's face. I looked to make sure everything was as I requested and I leaned over and kissed my son. My husband and I took our seats on the front pew and receive the visitors as they came to view his body and pay their respects. It seemed like the people would not stop coming. I am beyond thankful for all of the outpouring of love that was shown that day. That undesirable pain returned and the tears flowed. Today I could not remember most of the people that were there. And then that gut-wrenching moment came when they closed the coffin and that was my final goodbye to my son Brian. On the trip to the cemetery, I just stared out the window. I just wanted this to be over. I wanted to go home. The rest of the day was a blur of people coming and going.

CHAPTER 18

The week after the funeral, I went most of the week without crying. Was this the victory I had been looking for? I felt pretty good and was able to stay composed even when my husband broke down. I was able to comfort him with composure. Even though I was able to comfort him, deep inside of me I wished he did not have these moments. I knew he was in so much pain, but I was trying to avoid feeling my pain. I felt as though I was getting stronger. This was the woman I knew myself to be… strong and able to endure. I realized later on that on a deeper level; I was not allowing myself to think about Brian and deal with my grief. It was just surface thoughts, and that was easier to deal with. If my feelings attempted to go beyond the surface, I quickly diverted the thought and brought it back to the surface. I was able to function and move on but my life was never going to be the same. For a few weeks after the funeral, I very seldom cried. I provided comfort and encouragement to my husband, who was struggling daily. But to my surprise, the tears were helpful for his healing. At this particular time avoidance was helpful for my healing. I thought about Brian daily but I just did not let myself cry. When I did cry, I felt like I was losing control and control is the one thing I did not want to lose. I did not want to sink into a state of depression. It has been so many years since I had suffered from depression and did not want to go down that road again. The one thing I did was dedicated more of my time strengthening my relationship with God. I was not angry with God. I did not understand, but I was not angry. I still had a desire to worship God, and I believed the only way I was going to survive this was with the help of God. And I began writing little poems or just special words to Brian.

> *I want to hug you one more time*
> *I want to tell you I love you one more time*
> *I want to just talk with you one more time*
> *I want to just sit and watch you one more time*
> *I want to hear your dreams one more time*

I can think of so many things I want to share
  with you just one more time
But instead, I have all the special memories
  that
I can reflect on over and over again and smile
  one more time.

This was part of my therapy. When I felt myself slipping into that dark hole, I would start praying and then I would write. I had to find ways to avoid the crying. My husband told me that he wanted to cry because it made him feel better. I started to understand that even though we both lost a child, the healing process was so very different for the both of us. We shared time together and talked through our feelings but a great deal of the healing we had to deal with in our own ways. Many people told me it was alright to cry, and that crying was good. But for me, crying did not seem to be good. When I did not cry I honestly felt like I was going to be all right. There was hope when there were no tears. When the tears came, I felt like there was no hope. Even when I talked with God, I avoided the tears. I could talk about Brian, think about Brian and comfort others when it pertained to Brian, and I was ok with all of that, as long as I did not cry.

Is That You Speaking To Me?

So many times I ask, "Is that you speaking to me?" When choosing a blouse to where and I hear you say Mom, you will look fierce with the blouse on!! Is that you speaking to me? When sitting at my desk at work and I hear you say Mom stop daydreaming and get back to work. When sitting on the edge of my bed and I hear you say Mom I love you Is that you speaking to me? I wait patiently for the moment to hear your voice, because it's always followed by your smile. I hold on to the belief that it is you speaking to me.

So my writing journey begins. It is so easy for me to put pen to paper and begin to express my feelings.

Life After Brian:
I stay so busy and never sat down and looked at my new life. My new painful reality – Life without Brian Every day I think of Brian and miss him But I try to divert my

attention from the sadness For fear of sinking into the black pit and never returning I can smile and laugh at the memories I can talk about him with a smile on my face But am I really living my new life? There is someone new in my life. He did not replace Brian. In fact He is not really new in my life. We just have a closer and more intimate relationship. He provides a contentment I have never felt. He provides the strength I need to keep living life after Brian. I call him Savior, I call him protector, But most of all, I call him Father. He is my comfort in my new life And He has shown me how to live life after Brian.

I can do all things through Christ, which strengthens me. Philippians 4:13

This therapy did not last long because I could not think. I was always good at writing poems and was always very creative but I was drawing a blank. Nothing would come. I could not pull any of my thoughts together. I also could no longer complete reading a book. I was an avid reader. I would read a book in a week and enjoy reading but now I could not complete any book that I started. I was changing and not realizing that the death of my son played a major role in this change. I became so disorganized and often got confused and frustrated when trying to complete a task. I am usually a very organized person, but I was all over the place. I would come home from work, eat dinner and go upstairs and get in the bed. I used to get home, eat and get in my office and get back to work on various personal projects I was working on but I lost interest. I lost interest in my web design business. I kept a few customers but refused to take on any new customers. I even contemplated closing my business. Everything was so overwhelming and my only desire was to go to bed watch television until I fell asleep. Through all of this I never tried to figure out why, nor did I care. I could not sleep through the night any longer. And I was always awake at 5:30 every morning. I thought about Brian every day but I was ok and there were no tears. I lost my drive and was just content with existing.

    Depression was successful at taking control of me. That is the funny thing about depression; it can easily sneak up on you and consume you. I started having anxiety attacks. I could not see that light at the end of the tunnel. If I could, I would sleep all day. It became a struggle to get up for work in the morning and I really did not want to be around people. I did not want to talk to anyone about my feelings. I was sitting at my desk one day at work and I could not get Brian out of my head. I stopped what I was doing, and I just sat at my desk with Brian on my mind. I became so overwhelmed. I asked my friend Stacey to meet me in the bathroom because I needed someone to talk to and I had a meltdown. Stacey was so sweet and understanding. She allowed me to release my tears and pain. There were many other moments like this but I would go out to my car and have my private meltdowns. At times like this, you feel like you need someone but you don't want to be a burden to others. I thought about seeing my doctor but I did not want to go back on medication. Anti-depression medication gave me a cloudy drugged up feeling and that was not what I wanted at the time.

So the first thing I needed to recognize that I was depressed. I knew the source this time, but I needed a game plan to get myself out of this funk. Time to open up the Word of God and rely totally on Him to pull me through. I prayed and prayed some more. I began a fast to seek out God. I was seeking God and looking for what good was to come from this tragedy. And my answer came; help others find hope that are experiencing the loss of a child.

I started getting frustrated with people saying, "I

know how you feel, I lost my aunt" or "I know how you feel, I lost my mother". Not to diminish anyone's lost, but it is not the same. I lost my mother, and it was devastating but not the same. I had a desire to be around other parents that understood my pain. I started looking for support groups. I found quite a few support groups but only one specific to parents that have lost a child. The location and time were not convenient.

I begin thinking about starting my own support group. I researched starting a 501C3 and became overwhelmed with all that it entails and decided this is probably not for me. I went into prayer mode and I felt like God was telling me that I needed to do this. So I got back online and began my research again. I came across an organization (Bereaved Parents of the USA) that caught my interest. This is a national organization and there was a link on their website to start a chapter. Was this my way to getting started with a support group? I submitted my request to start a chapter. I got a response explaining the process, and a roadblock presented itself. One stipulation was that in order to start a chapter you needed to be a parent that has lost a child and it has to be more than 18 months since your child has passed. Well, this was only two months after Brian passed. I responded to the email thanking them and expressed my interest in doing this in the near future. I explained that it had only been 2 months. I was then asked to tell my story. I sent an email explaining my loss and why I wanted to start this chapter and I was approved. I did not want to sit around and wallow in my pain. I knew that there would be many parents walking in my shoes and I wanted to provide hope for them. I wanted them to know that they could go on and remember and cherish the memories of their child. I knew that I was not healed, or that I was magically alright but I did have a need to help others.

Hopelessness is one of the most overwhelming emotions that you feel when you lose a child and I needed to provide hope. I needed others to see how God was working in my life and know where I draw my comfort and strength from. This was the project I needed to help me move forward. I still hurt and not a day goes by that I do not think about Brian. The support group became an important part of my healing process. I was on the Board of Managers at the William Emslie YMCA and I spoke to the Executive Director, Danielle Roberts, about holding our monthly meetings at the YMCA. She graciously provided a room at the YMCA for our monthly meetings. Our meetings fluctuated monthly. My husband got a little discouraged because there were not many people who came. I explained to him that it was more important for us to be there every month just in case someone needed to talk. We have two parents and a grandmother that come consistently and we get occasional drop-ins. Our purpose is to be there when the need arises. Being able to share with others who have experienced the same loss is gratifying because we can gain insight on how each of us deals differently with their grief.

We hold an Annual Candle Lighting Banquet to remember our children and this is all part of my therapy. Brian is a daily constant part of me and his memory will live on. Helping others is helping me. I will continue to inspire hope in any way that the Lord will lead me.

CHAPTER 19

Death is final but your grief is an ongoing evolution born out of your love for the deceased. It is necessary to go through the grief process because it is extremely important to progress through the process. I am not saying that progression means healing. Absolutely not, but progression means learning how and finding ways to deal with your grief. There are many options to consider such as group counseling, support groups, your church, books, etc. I think everyone has a different need, and it is important to find the right plan.

Early on in the grief process, it might be difficult to think about a plan. I believe during this time, live out your emotions; be angry, question God, blame someone, question yourself, etc. Get these out of your system because they will become a hindrance in your grief journey. And definitely, do not try to avoid your feelings and emotions because they will eventually come crashing down on you. Be prepared to hear all the cliché sayings; I know how you must feel, you will get over it in time, well at least you have other children, etc. Believe me, after hearing these so often you become angry and you just wish that people would say nothing at all.

When grieving the loss of a child, there can be long-term effects on the emotional stability of the parent. That is why working through your grief is very important. Along with hopeless comes the question, "what is my purpose in life?"

Part of my recovery was rediscovering who I was and what God's purpose was for my life. I say rediscovered because the day Brian died, my life changed forever. There are several steps in the grief journey. The first step is an awareness of your loss. Denial is very common during your grief journey. It is important to accept the reality of your loss. This will open you up to get in touch with your feelings and emotions. During denial, you may feel emotionless and unfocused. The next step is working through your feelings and emotions. Do not try to bury what you feel; cry, scream and do what you need to do. The next step is adjusting to your loss. Find ways to continuing living and integrating the loss into your life. Redefine your life if necessary and most of all take care of yourself. So many times grief can morph into physical and mental ailments. Make sure you are eating and getting enough rest. If you notice any physical or mental changes, make sure you seek medical attention. It is important to take care of yourself to be able to move through your grief journey. Of course, this is all easier said than done.

I found my health and eating habits suffer during my grief journey. I continue to struggle with health-related issues but I am showing progress. I had to first realize that these things that were going on with me were indirectly related to my grief. I think we all mentally prepare ourselves for the loss of our parents, possible loss of a sibling, a friend, a relative but I don't think our minds wrap around the thought of losing a child. The death of a child creates a pain that is unique to the individual parent. An unexpected death can be extremely devastating. It is like you have been blindsided. Initially, there is numbness and shock. Especially if your child met with a violent death, you find your sorrow and anger too great for you to bear. You feel devastatingly guilty at not having been able to protect your child, however improbable such thoughts might be. You feel extremely helpless and powerless. The complexity and confusion of your feelings may even convince you that you are "going crazy." I know after hearing all of this, you wonder how am I supposed to have hope? It is not easy, but it is possible. You just have to find the right game plan to implement for this journey.

CHAPTER 20

Today I still think of Brian daily and constantly. There is no dark cloud that consumes my life. I am not perfect or where I want to be but there has been great progress. I still can't sleep the whole night through. I still have moments where it is hard to focus. But I can say I have hope and I have a God who is with me every step of the way.

Who is the new me? I am the woman who refuses to let depression find a home in me. I am the woman who will use her pain to help others. I am the woman who prays daily. I don't know what other valleys I will have to endure, but I know I will not face them alone.

Dutch Evangelist, Corrie Ten Boom quotes, "The measure of a life, after all, is not its duration, but it's donation." I am looking to donate and make an impact.

That is part of my new mission. Share my experience and inspire hope in others. This is the new me and I am aware of the journey ahead of me.

Many think the mention of Brian's name will bring tears and sadness, but I am here to tell you that the mention of his name brings so much joy to my heart. Underneath all the new me, I am still Brian Matthew Spruill's mother.

My Prayer:

> *Heavenly Father, I come before you as a humble servant. I thank you for all you have done, are doing and will do. Thank you for being the light on that dark and lonely road. Thank you for carrying me when I was too weak to walk. Thank you for being that ear when no one else would listen. When I am traveling down the road of destruction, thank you for picking me up and recalculating my direction. Thanks for your unconditional love. But most of all thank you for your grace and mercy when I am so undeserving. Amen*

www.ingramcontent.com/pod-product-compliance
Lightning Source LLC
Chambersburg PA
CBHW071150090426
42736CB00012B/2294